HEARTBREAK TO HOPE

Heartbreak to Hope

Poems of Support for Grief and Loss
by

KARA BOWMAN

Adelaide Books
New York / Lisbon
2021

HEARTBREAK TO HOPE
Poems of Support for Grief and Loss
By Kara Bowman

Published by Adelaide Books, New York / Lisbon
adelaidebooks.org
Editor-in-Chief
Stevan V. Nikolic

For any information, please address Adelaide Books
at info@adelaidebooks.org
or write to:
Adelaide Books
244 Fifth Ave. Suite D27
New York, NY, 10001

ISBN: 978-1-954351-78-3

Printed in the United States of America

*For Doug, Janna, Adra and Tory, who taught me how to love,
and Bruno and Lupita, who gave me more people to love.*

Contents

Introduction

I was sitting in a comfortable chair across from an impeccably dressed, petite, white-haired woman. She was crying gently as she described her husband's death and the sharp pain she felt in her heart whenever she thought of him. She suddenly paused, looked me straight in the eye, and plaintively said, "I just don't know what to do. I don't know how to grieve."

An hour later, a soft-spoken, intelligent young Latino man was in the same spot describing the agony of his life without his mother in it. His face looked desperate as he asked me, "Will this get better? What should I be doing?"

In my work as a grief therapist, I often receive these heartfelt questions. I wrote this poetry collection as a response to my clients and every person who wonders how to help themselves through the difficult process of grief. There are many things to learn but the most important thing to know is that grief is not something we need to *do*; it is something we simply need to *allow*. If we feel our feelings without judgment, bathed in self-compassion and allowing in compassion from others, the sharp edges will soften with time.

This collection grew out of the many hours I have spent with people who are mourning every imaginable type of loss, as well as my own experiences of grief. I tried to capture what

I have heard: the expected emotions, such as sadness, longing and pain, and the sometimes surprising emotions, like numbness, anger and relief. My reflections are offered in bite-sized pieces, each capturing one part of the kaleidoscope-like experience of bereavement, allowing you to take in as much or as little as you choose at one time.

We mourn both acutely alone and invisibly connected to everyone who has ever lived and grieved. In these poems, I hope to name some things you are experiencing and may not yet have words for. I also hope to help you recognize parts of your inner world that you didn't realize existed. Finally, I hope that, as you read these poems, you will know others have felt similar things and you will feel less alone.

While it is now known that there are no set stages of grief, the poems are organized broadly in terms of some common reactions. The first section reflects when the wound is new, the second when grief has settled in for a long visit, and the third when adjustment to a new reality begins to take hold. As you read, you should find some recognition and comfort in these pages. Like the two clients described above, my wish is for you to ultimately arrive at a place of acceptance, peace and love.

ACT ONE

Everything is the same,
but nothing is familiar.
I am plucked from the life I am living,
And ushered into another world entirely.
> Not knowing the rules,
> not understanding how things function,
> not knowing what to do.
I am in uncharted territory because
> just as every person is unique,
> every grief is unique, too.
Nobody knows how to act,
> what to say,
> and when to say nothing in this bizarre world.
There are strange forms to fill out
> and equipment to return
> and clothing to sort through
> and estates to settle.
Nobody asked for this existence and nobody wants it.
And yet, here I am,
> in this world without a solid ground,
> in this world where things keep moving,
> in this world with new places, like the mortuary,
> and new tasks, like writing an obituary.
The people are different and weird.
> Not the same ones as before.
> They talk about donating organs.

And bring Yule logs in July.

And ask about power of attorney.

I want my normal back:

    my morning coffee on the back porch,

    my minor irritation when I'm running low on gas,

    my one and only love.

I want to go home to the world I knew.

The Line

There will always be before and after,
An impenetrable line between them.
I can see the other side,
but I cannot visit.
I was there
and now I'm here.
Throat choking,
Wanting yesterday back.

Hope

The beagle is pacing,
waiting,
looking up expectantly every so often,
lying down trying to rest, lightly,
jumping at every sound,
running to the door,
hoping to see the recognizable shape,
hear the familiar voice,
smell the comforting aroma,
and feel the gentle hand,
like nobody else's.

The Heart

A gaping wound pierces my heart in the shape of my beloved.
Someday it will scab over.
Someday,
far, far in the future,
it will turn into scar tissue.
I will rub it and it will be soft and smooth and comforting.
It will be with me,
in the shape of my love,
for as long as I live.

The Gang

A gang has made itself at home inside of me.
The angry punk teenager inside my head,
pounding to her music.
The tense office worker in my throat,
tightening to control the chaos.
The heavy lethargic convalescent in my chest,
wanting only to close his eyes and sink into the bed.
The small boy who misses his mother behind my eyes,
with pressure mounting to the point of overwhelm.
The marathon runner in my legs,
twitching and energized even after the race has been run.
And the baby in my gut,
kicking me,
wanting only to get out.

Today

Today half of my heart was seized from my chest,
leaving my body to sob with what is left.
Screaming and protesting,
eyes saturated and painfully swollen,
wailing "No!" into the ether.

She cannot move.
Not even the twitch of a muscle.
She lies,
the earth pulling her like a magnet.
She feels like there's a wet wool blanket on her chest,
making it hard to breathe.
Her heart is ballast, weighting her down.
Standing up seems as impossible as a newborn walking.
Every cell in her body is depleted,
like prey who has escaped the puma.
Without even enough energy to think
about what has happened.
Wanting to sleep and sleep,
timelessly,
into the past.

The Ride

Trapped in an unsteady roller coaster car,
click, click, clicking toward the top,
I feel every bump in my spine.
I hurtle downward, screaming, with my eyes tightly shut.
Every muscle in my body is straining. Against what?
The sharp turn takes my breath away,
and then we lurch upward again,
before another drop dislodges my stomach to my throat.
Then peace.
But only for a moment as I descend into the spiral,
disoriented.
I ride the gentle ups and downs,
emerging on jelly legs.

Right Now

He wanted a celebration of life.
Right now, I want a funeral.
I don't want to celebrate and be grateful;
I want to wail.
I don't want to put on a happy face.
I don't want to remember the good times.
It's not time for acceptance;
it's time for protest.
It's too soon to think about the beauty of life.
Right now, I'm mourning death.
Later,
when my pain is purged,
I will celebrate his life.

The Haven

A crack appears in time,
a tiny child wedges into it
held tightly in a soft warm refuge,
snug and protected,
surrounded by peace.

Food

A steaming bowl of pasta...
Warm French toast with sweet syrup...
A perfect fruit salad, without too many melons.

Food used to be so gloriously enticing.

People bring
homemade samosas...
fresh rustic bread...
rich chicken soup.

To comfort.

I don't care anymore.
My stomach is indifferent.
Numb to pleasure.
Unavailable.
Preoccupied with mourning.

The Question

Why?
My mind repeats this word endlessly.
Why?
My mind thinks it can figure it out.
Why?
My mind tries every angle and,
when it runs out of angles,
it loops back to the beginning,
and goes over well-trodden territory yet again.

Why?
My mind thinks it must understand
how this has happened,
who is to blame,
which story makes sense.
How else will I have peace?

But maybe, I tell my mind, you don't have to know.
And maybe, I tell it, you can have peace without a story,
by accepting what is,
just as it is,
without any explanations.
My mind is intrigued by the idea, but unsure.
I let my mind sit with the beautiful possibility
of not asking why.

Love

Take good care of your precious pain.
Wrap your strong arms around it.
Hold it against your warm chest.
Rock it gently,
telling it softly that it is loved.
It is needed.
It is important.
It makes perfect sense.
And love it, just as it is,
in all of its agonizing beauty.

The Movie

The movie rolls in my head,
always stopping at that scene.
You know the one.
The one that was so intense I closed my eyes,
and put my head in my lap,
and hugged my arms tightly around myself.
I was beside you, but not with you.
Frozen in that scene.
The movie kept rolling even as I stopped time.
Maybe I should find out what happens next.
But not yet.

Unbalanced

An oriole in a tornado
Swirling
Twisting
Twirling
Spinning
Churning
Never steady for a moment
Always in motion
Not sure which way is up
Or when it will end

The Long Goodbye

They call it the long goodbye,
which only kind of fits.

It's not just one long, aching send-off;
it's also a never-ending repetition of smaller departures.
Goodbye to his remembering what we did today.
Goodbye to his ability to make his own appointments.
Goodbye to leaving him alone in the house.
Goodbye to his ability to think clearly.
Goodbye to him ever being able to talk again.

Finally, after my wounded heart has
already grieved a thousand pains,
it is goodbye to his warm, familiar body itself.

Serenity

A solitary drip on a verdant pond breaks the quiet,
and then silence.
Deep silence.
All muscles can stand down,
melt toward the earth,
no sense of movement,
only deep relaxation.
From the farthest stars
resting in the night sky
to the deepest bones
buried beneath skin and muscle,
at peace and at rest.

Remembering

I go over every detail obsessively.
I am terrified of forgetting
your walk,
your impish smile when making puns,
the feel of your arm around my shoulders.
I want to freeze my memories,
so they remain sharp and clear.
Forever.

Nerves

Raw nerves
aching for quiet, for soothing,
but none to be had.
Just more of the same cacophony.
of jarring noise
and pain.
Heart stripped bare
of its protections.
Muscles at the ready
to propel legs to run.
Adrenaline cursing.
Brain firing,
activated.
Always on alert
and aware
something is wrong.

Overcast

Gray
Leaden
Dusky
Faint
Dull
Heavy
Dismal
Ashen
Dim
Are the colors still there behind the fog?

The House of Horrors

My grief is a house of horrors,
a funhouse in name only.
There are sudden twists as I am jerked
from one direction to another.
Here a macabre clown intones a hollow laugh;
there an otherworldly ghost moans.
I don't remember choosing to get on this ride.
I wait, abiding, until I see the sun again.

Where Did You Go?

Where did you go?
You were just here.
I feel you here, but you're not.
Not really.
Are you somewhere else?
Where are you?
Are you ephemeral or eternal?
Are you embodied or an essence?
Are you happy?
Are you at peace?
Will you let me know?
Please?

Crazy

The situation is crazy, not me.
I keep telling myself that,
but it doesn't feel true.
What is crazy if it is not being untethered from reality?
Crazy is fighting with the truth.
I used to pity people who had
uncontrollable and inexplicable bursts of emotion.
Now that's me.
I can't remember whether I ate breakfast,
or paid a bill,
or returned a friend's phone call.
I can't remember how I felt yesterday
or what I used to think.
Crazy is having my mind rule me
rather than me calling the shots.
What does it mean
to be sane in an insane situation?
Maybe it means believing
that my reactions make sense,
even if I can't figure out how.
What doesn't make sense is what happened,
not me.

Numb

Numb is a feeling.
Some say it is not, but I know it is.
It is strong and steel gray.
Edgy and dull at the same time.
Not hard, not soft.
Not dark, not light.
Empty, yet very much alive.

Distance

I hover above in a corner of the ceiling,
watching the pain pour from the people below.
Strangely there,
and strangely not.

The Big Waves

They say you can surf the big waves if you know how.
The trick isn't in fancy techniques above water.
The secret is to hold your breath under water
for an entire wave.
The time seems interminable,
the depth unnavigable.
But, with practice,
a person can endure and resurface.

The real danger is in two or three waves
right on top of each other.
Staying down is the only way.
Waiting,
not until you are done,
but until the waves are done with you.
Settling into the peace of the deep wetness.
Conserving energy
for your eventual swim to the surface,
where the sun will make itself known once again.

The Unknown

The ambiguousness of the in-between,
standing with a foot on each plank,
trying not to fall in.
Wanting to know,
to say, "Yes, that's it",
no matter what "it" is.
What is known
is that all will never be known.
And that will have to be enough.

Fudge

He always watches his diet carefully,
eating salads in restaurants,
and measuring out half the meal for a doggie bag.

Today he ordered vanilla ice cream with fudge.
Then, when the waitress came,
he asked for another little pitcher of fudge on the side.

Today he wanted ice cream with fudge
and a little pitcher of fudge on the side.

Today he buried his wife.

The Lake

I look out over the lake
peering to see something, anything, through the fog.
The fog obscures everything that is normally there:
The water, the birds, the opposite shore.
There are no trees, no boats, no brush visible,
only damp gray air,
making the world small and faint.
Someday the fog will lift.
It will, won't it?

The Grocery Store

Going to the grocery store feels like a solo ascent of Everest.
I go over endless details again and again.
I finally get up the courage to open the front door.
I am committed, but afraid.
Hoping not to break down next to the cereal.
Hoping not to see someone who knows.
Hoping not to see someone who doesn't know,
so I have to explain.
Hoping, above all, not to let my insides show
so I look normal.

I am somehow making my way through the maze of aisles
when I see his favorite cookies.
I turn my eyes and move on quickly,
not wanting to linger and let emotions immobilize me.
I backtrack several times,
unwittingly passing things that are just
where they have always been.
(How is that possible?)

Finally, my list is done.
I go to the checkout line and,
with my last remaining energy,
tell the clerk I found everything,
and yes, I do want a bag,
and no, I don't need help out.

I get into my car and close the door.
Driving blindly home,
where I collapse into the nearest chair.
I made it.

The Loss

We are each grieving the same loss
and yet
when it flew into my body
and flew into your body
it changed shape
so you can never completely know my loss
and I can never completely know yours.
And yet
I can cradle your loss as I cradle my own,
and you can cradle mine along with yours,
as we rock together,
with each of our losses
the same
and yet
distinct.

Hospital Sounds

Whoosh, whoosh.
Beep, beep.
The background track to despair.
Whoosh, whoosh.
Beep, beep.
With an occasional piercing alarm
or doctor's voice
as punctuation.
Whoosh, whoosh.
Beep, beep.
Going on and on,
until it doesn't.
And silence says
what the sounds kept at bay:
that the fight is over now
and the sorrow has begun.

The Earth

The earth started a new orbit.
There was no explosion.
No flash of light.
No boom.
It just quietly slipped into its new trajectory,
rounding the sun,
on a path that didn't exist yesterday.
I expected a change this monumental to
be marked by a din like no other.
Instead there was silence,
as the earth changed forever,
which doesn't seem right.

The Preemie

Born into the world before she was ready.
Tiny and fragile.
A finger touching her a bit too hard leaves a bruise.
Her skin can tear,
sights are too strong,
sounds too loud.
She curls into a ball and waits.

Chaos

Buildings loom above.
Cars race by
in and out.
People walk
every which way.
Sounds of radios and cars blend together
to create a background
punctuated by endless horns and sirens and beeping.
Storefronts vie for attention with their
bright and blinking colors.
Babies cry, dogs bark, near and far.

There is no oasis of calm.

No

Every cell is in pain.
Sharp, throbbing agony.
Everything hurts.
A forceful, intense ache.
The body is screaming out
NO!

ACT TWO

The Wind

The wind is calm but relentless.
It picks up leaves and swirls them around lazily.
They tumble in the air, every which way.
The tree branches shake, slightly but steadily.
The grass blades tremble, ceding to the wind.
The birds silently adjust their flight to
acknowledge the force of nature.
The bushes dance indifferently, unable to resist.

My Phone

My phone doesn't ping
with the joke that was just between us
and the small doses of love
you gave me all throughout the day.

My heart still jumps a bit
every time I hear the chime
hoping, thinking
it might be you.

But then I remember,
and the dismay washes through me,
because it will never be you again.

Some People

Some people have never been to this place,
but think they know what the vistas look like.
Others have been here
but let me describe the scenery for myself.
Ones I have known all my life
sometimes have knowing nods,
but they don't know.
Others who I don't know well
can sit with me,
understanding the anguish,
because they, too, have seen through these eyes.
A web of connections
creates a vast invisible alliance.
I never knew it existed
and now I am part of it.
Grateful to know there are others who comprehend.

The Beach

Fog descends on the beach like the ashes from a fire,
choking out the sun.
The water churns and undulates,
while beside it the sand calmly sits and waits.

The Path

I am on a journey to an unknown destination.
A journey I never wanted.
A journey I never requested.
A journey I never consented to.
Yet, here I am.

I look down and see a path
but I don't know where it will take me.
I find myself in the middle of a thick, dark forest.
I keep walking.
I emerge to see a mountain before me.
I don't want to climb it, but know I must,
since I can't go back and don't want to stay here forever.
I can still see the path,
but I don't know how long it is.
I scale the mountain and enter a meadow.
I want to rest here but my legs keep walking.
At the edge of the meadow, I see another forest.
My path twists and turns,
rises and falls.
I don't know what is ahead.
I only know that I must keep walking.

The Stones

The little girl watches the stones as they
tumble over and over in the chamber.
They hit each other,
with sharp clicks.
She doesn't like the sound.
She doesn't like the chaos of the movement.
She doesn't like the violence of their collisions.
She believes, though,
that if she can abide this phase that she doesn't like,
the sounds will soften
and the gems will emerge polished and beautiful someday.

The Caregiver

Caregiver.
It's a title I never asked for but gladly took on.
I heard the word at every appointment.
Who's the Caregiver?
I'd like to talk to the Caregiver.
Are you the Caregiver?

It's a role I slipped into easily.
It seemed natural,
even as it grew and grew,
and eventually took over all else.
I was proud to do it,
and I did a damn good job.

I learned how to change a dressing,
and give an injection.
I could cajole a spoonful of applesauce
into a reluctant mouth,
wipe a sweaty brow,
and change a bed with someone in it.
I knew when to read aloud,
when to sit silently,
and when to gently reassure with a touch.

Now my role is done.
Gone in an instant,

and I am lost
trying to remember who I was before,
when Caregiver was only another word.

Color Show

Deep dark blue.
Almost black.
Slowly changing into light blue.
Morphing into green.
And then yellow.
Deeper and deeper.
To sunset orange.
Glowing in the sky.
Shifting to red.
And slowly to pink.
Back to blue.
Mostly deep dark blue.

His Heart

His heart finally grasps what it has always known.
The losses,
and the holes where losses should have been.
Now he sees clearly
what he had
and what he never had.
He is mourning it all.

Ungrieved Losses

My ungrieved losses have piled up
throughout my life.
I was too young to know how to grieve
when Sierra died.
Nobody taught me.
We got a new dog
and I learned to move on.
I was too scared to grieve
when my trust was ripped from me
and my autonomy violated
a few years later.
I didn't know I should grieve
when I moved and lost all of my friends.
I thought it was just part of life and,
after all,
I chose it,
so why would I cry?
And then,
when my tia died,
I was too busy with my job and kids.
I didn't have time to give myself up
to sweet sadness.
After all, self-control is a virtue,
isn't it?
Why would I want to suffer?
Now I have lost another love and,

when I opened the basement door
to add it to the pile,
my lifetime of ungrieved wounds let me know
that they are there, too,
waiting,
patiently,
to be mourned.

Green

Agitation,
noise,
unpredictability,
all around me.

So I slip out
into the green expanse,
the grass tickling my neck,
and the leaves swaying gently above me
like a thousand mothers rocking their babies.
Clouds lazily stroll across the sky
while a starling circles nonchalantly,
held aloft almost effortlessly by the wind.

Surrounded by soothing,
I immerse myself.

What to Do

It's difficult to know what to do

when the world changes in an instant,
when the land is alien,
when there are so many things to figure out,
when there's no understanding,
when there are so many people to support,
when knees are buckling,
when thoughts are cloudy and vague,
when nothing looks familiar,
when all energy has suddenly vanished,

when the person who could best help me through this
is the very one who is gone.

Your Things

The green wool ski hat,
the Labrador mug from your brother,
the blue plaid shirt,
the phone with my picture on it,
the dented Dodge Ram you loved so much,
the worn leather boots,
the box of cereal, half-eaten,
the flat pillow that you folded over.
My heart aches because I have everything
except you.

The Moan

I hear a sound,
a low moan,
off in the distance.
I can't make out which direction.
It sounds somber,
desolate,
lonely,
It wails on and on
in a deep lament.

I think it is coming from me.

Who Are You?

Are you the type that breaks down crying,
or the type that is calm in a crisis?
Are you the sort who is overwhelmed by feelings,
or do you have trouble detecting where they live in you?
Is this about the truth of what is inside you,
or protecting other people's insides with your placid exterior?
Does your head tell you it was a good
death so you should be grateful,
while your heart screams it doesn't care
how good it was, it's still all wrong?
Does the finality seem unbelievable?
Do the memories seem unreal?
Are the details becoming fuzzier and further away?
Are you angry at things like genetic predispositions?
Are you alone or inundated with people?
Is that comforting or draining?
Is your body a stranger to you,
with new aches and appetites?
Or is your body your best friend and a refuge?
Are you holding onto thoughts and feelings like a lifeline?
Or are you reeling with the ever-changing
confusion of uncertainty?
Do you even know who you are,
not for all time,
but right in this moment?

Little Comforts

The warmth of a heating pad,
a raspberry bursting in my mouth,
the sun on my face,
remembering his puns,
sinking into my favorite chair,
smelling his favorite shirt,
sledding on a sunny day,
my cat settled into my lap,
rubbing a sore muscle,
hearing you talk about my love.

The Thaw

She is exhausted.
She has put off feeling for so long,
in order to cook,
to comfort,
to make sure no appointment was missed,
no pillow unfluffed,
no whisper unheard.
Her heart has been in a deep freeze,
and now it is thawing.
It aches,
it despairs,
it has so much to feel,
to process.

But mostly, it is just so very tired.

Should I Have?

Should I have done something different?
The thought is always there.
Sometimes it screams.
Sometimes it whispers.
Sometimes it lists the things I could have done.
It is blocking my path so I can't walk down the trail.
I can't even see the trail around it.
I just want to find the answer that will let me move past it.
I want to stop the nagging thought,
the haunting sound.
But I can't,
so I scream back, "Leave me alone!"
Or I whisper a plea,
"Not now. Please, not now."
But it will not budge
no matter what I do.
Until I befriend it.
Only when I am no longer at war with it, does it soften.
Only then does it yield.
No answers are forthcoming,
and it is still there,
but it steps aside
and allows me to move down the path nonetheless.

Fading

The last glow softly fades on the horizon,
I can still make out the line of mountains in the distance,
until I wonder whether I am seeing them,
or just imagining what was there before.
My heart clenches suddenly,
as I try to remember exactly where the line was,
and what it looked like in the majesty of the full sun,
frantic that someday I won't be able to recall it at all.

What Is Lost

What is lost is all that we shared together, of course,
but that lives on forever in my memory.
Even more painful to give up are the parts
that lived only in her memory.
Her last year of high school,
her secret recipe for gazpacho,
her love for her grandfather,
the history of every plant in the garden;
these are lost forever,
and will never be known again.

Regret

Little gremlins nipping at my heels,
chasing my every thought.
impervious to reason,
or requests of mercy.
The path in my brain well-worn.
Thinking that by beating myself up,
I can make things right.
I can turn back time.
With enough effort,
I can put the fractured vase together again.
It sneaks up on me.
I turn around and there it is.
Some of it tightly wound to thoughts,
some of it unattached and floating free.
"What if?"
Two of the hardest words.
They hide,
coiled,
only to strike again.

The Truth

Do I have to feel bad?
I never really liked him.
If I don't feel bad, am I a horrible person?
The truth is, he was mean to me.
The truth is, he was selfish.
The truth is, I'm not sorry he's gone.
Does this make me awful?
As bad as he was?
I'm supposed to turn the other cheek,
but the other cheek is bruised, too.
I'm not mad any more.
But it's a sad thing when someone's life is not missed.
And, the truth is, I don't miss him.

The Casket

My son is in the casket.
I want to crawl in beside him.
I want to go where he is going.
Anything to be with him.
Anything to stop this world from going on without him.

But then I hear my son say,
ever so faintly,
please,
for me,
live your life,
and don't get into this casket with me.

You Were There

You were always there,
weaving in and out of my day,
like my breath,
making contact,
and disappearing again,
but I knew by your little loves,
that the big love was there,
hidden, just out of sight.

The Swamp

The swamp
Is dark under the thick canopy of cypress
with tendrils everywhere in the water
shiny water
reflecting green all around
so that there is no difference between land and air.

I did not know
until this moment
that I knew how to swim.

Teeter-Totter

Back and forth,
Back and forth,
like a teeter-totter.
But this is no game.
This is real.
Relief, then guilt,
Relief, then guilt.
Caught in the repetition.
Neither side can give up first.
So it keeps going,
Up and down,
Up and down.
With no end in sight.

Not Knowing

Will I ever feel good again?
I don't know.
Is it a betrayal to feel okay?
Is there an appropriate amount of time?
Is laughing not honoring a life,
or is it what I am supposed to do?
I want an instruction sheet,
so all I have to do is follow the steps.
Because not knowing is far worse.

Nowhere to Go

The people are streaming along the sidewalks
at breakneck speed,
weaving and jostling,
to get there faster.

I used to have places to go
in a rush,
moving with purpose,
instinctually,
to arrive at places familiar
and new.

Now I watch others out the window,
longingly.

I have nowhere to go.

Everything Is Funny

Everything is funny.

A human being is gone from this earth,
and she is concerned about her potato salad.

He expired the same day his credit card did.

I need the death certificate to get power of attorney,
and power of attorney to get a birth certificate,
and the birth certificate to get the death certificate.

The customer service rep made a mistake
and now I have to prove I'm not dead,
on paper.
Showing up in person is not considered proof.

Death is hilarious.

Yarn

Yarn jumbled in a mess of strings so tight
that it will never be untangled.
I don't know how long it is.
I don't know how it got this way.
I don't know what the inside looks like.
I can't even find one end
to start the process of unraveling.
Do I have the will to start, one little snarl at a time?
Is it worth beginning when it seems endless?
Does any small part of me believe
that I'll be able to knit a beautiful sweater with it someday?

Change

He doesn't want to change.
How would she recognize him if he did?
He feels safe staying the same,
keeping the pillows on the couch the same,
holding onto her coat
for dear life.
What if she needs everything to be the same?
He knows that's silly but he can't let go.
What if he needs everything to be the same?
He'd better stay put.
He'd better not change.

Righteous Anger

He is angry.

Others get to grieve what they lost,
He has to grieve what he never got to have.

Others assume;
they apply their template to him.

He feels alone in his grief,
unique, different, wrong.

He is grieving his truth incognito,
afraid, sometimes, to even whisper it to himself.

Not speaking his reality aloud,
for fear others wouldn't understand,
or think kindly of him,
their compassion withering,

if they were to hear his truth.

Figuring Out

Her mind tries to grasp what it cannot.
It turns the same facts over and over again.
Looking for sense,
Looking for a pattern,
Looking for order,
Where there is none.

Letting Go

Settling into the present moment,
letting go completely,
not demanding to control,
that which cannot be controlled.

Peace,
not for the world,
and not forever,
just for this body at this time.

What I Lost

I lost so many things in one moment.
Practical things,
like knowing where to find the extra car keys.
Irreplaceable things,
like remembering who was at that birthday party in the rain.
Ideas,
like trust.
Roles.
Hopes.
Security.
My support system.
I lost so many things in one moment.
Shattered.
Never to be put back together the same way.

Don't

Don't tell me I'm going to grow from this.
Don't bring me flowers and platitudes.
I'm mad.
Don't make that wrong.

Don't bring me chicken soup and tell me I should eat more.
Right now,
I'm not hungry.

Don't tell me to be happy for all of
the wonderful things I had.
I don't have them anymore.
I don't feel happy.

But do come with openness,
ready to listen,
or to be silent.
Come for whatever is, right now.

Thanksgiving

It is Thanksgiving, it could not be stopped.
Yesterday, she made his favorite apple pie,
the one they always ate together after the big meal,
and snuck another piece of before bed.
Today, she is alone.
She sits down with the whole pie
and begins to eat.

Night

Night used to be my friend.

Now it is cold,
and mocks my inability to sleep.

Night used to be my friend.
We cuddled, laughing when the dog nosed his way in.
You ignored me, lost in a book.
We met in the middle for a goodnight peck.

I could always feel your body,
your warmth,
your breath
alongside me.

And I would be gently covered by the warm blanket of sleep,
knowing I was safe and loved.

Night used to be my friend,
When you were beside me.

The Concerned Face

People keep coming,
in ones, twos, threes.
Everyone has that face,
the concerned face.
It's always the same:
the furrowed brow,
the intense gaze,
the slightly pursed lips.
I'm seeing versions of it on old people,
young people,
delicate people,
strong people,
I mimic their faces,
except I have a tiny smile on my lips.

Out of Control

Words, words, ceaselessly,
every thought leads to another unrelated thought,
like a pachinko machine,
with lights flashing,
not knowing which path the ball will travel,
or where it will land.
It keeps bouncing and moving,
until it vibrates to rest.

Can't talk; no coherent thoughts,
brain moving slowly,
stuck in thick muck,
every expenditure of energy an effort.
It wants to be still.

Revving up, speeding,
slowing down, idling,
revving up, speeding,
slowing down, idling.

Crying Alone

I cry alone,
because others must not see me cry.
They don't know about us,
And wouldn't like it if they did.
So I am alienated
in my grief,
with the secret only we knew,
Of our strong and precious love.
It was as real as I am,
and always will be,
but now only I will know.

Remembering

Reminders are everywhere.
The Escher picture from your brother,
the shiny black dress shoes put neatly
back after the graduation party,
the walnut stool from that new shop downtown.
Each time I see one
an electrical charge surges through my heart
and my breath stops for just a moment.
I try to distract myself,
but then there's the calypso song in the movie,
the woodpecker on the on the tree out front,
or Tuscany in the book.
Sometimes I smell
your coat,
your sheets,
your shirt,
to remember,
on my own terms,
at my own time.

Complicated Trees

The ancient trees were beautiful from a distance,
with thick, green, sprawling canopies.

Now, standing beneath one,
beside its trunk,
I can see that the canopy is thin.

Under the green are complicated branches,
limbs crisscrossing each other
in impossibly complex tangles.
A messy maze of hard, rough wood,
holding up a façade of beauty.

The Cat

The cat is usually cuddly
but today, he has a gash in his paw.
The tabby doesn't want to do anything but lick the gash,
so he finds a place to hide where it's dark
and quiet and he can be alone.
He curls up on himself and tastes his wound,
attending to his pain,
waiting and licking and trusting,
that with patience and care,
someday the gash will heal,
and he will be okay again.

The Hut

I am walking,
trudging slowly,
and worrying with every step.
How will I keep going?
I want to stop.

There is a hut
where I can put my load down for the night,
and close my eyes,
and let the bed support my body.

And tomorrow I will walk again.
But I won't worry,
knowing a hut will appear,
maybe later than I would like,
but it will appear, all the same.

Hold Me Close

Wrap me in your warm arms.
Press my cheek against your heart.
Let me know you understand
these feelings I can't put words to.
Let me know you care
about my pain.
Rock me softly,
knowingly,
endlessly.
Love me through my anguish
by loving me through it.
It will gently melt in your embrace.

ACT THREE

The Story

So this is how the story ends.
I had no idea.
I tried to peer forward,
but could not see.
How many times did I wonder?
How many times did I torture myself trying to figure it out?
Even though I could not know.
But now I know.

Sunbeam

Thick, dark green cover of millions of leaves,
Knit together like a tightly woven blanket.

Mossy floor,
With patches of mud.

A tiny shaft of golden light reaches down,
Distant, but real.

The Wave

Unease
turns to concern.
Foreboding descends.
Apprehension takes hold
and flows into anxiety,
which morphs into dread
and progresses to full blown distress,
which leads to the intensity of panic
Crescendoing to terror.

Chaos is everywhere.

Slowly,
It begins to ebb.
Focused panic
melts to distress,
which softens to dread
and retreats to anxiety,
which lessens to apprehension,
that becomes foreboding,
which ebbs to concern
and comes to rest once again
on vague unease.

Floating

A tiny brown leaf sits on a larger green leaf,
Too small to stay aloft on its own,
They float together, drifting on the water,
Carried this way and that by the current,
Carried that way and this by the wind,
They lazily dance,
Gliding around and around,
Going nowhere and yet everywhere.

The Dive

She sits on the edge of the boat,
a tiny figure next to a huge churning ocean.
Will she fall?
Will she get pulled in?
Will something push her?
She feels terror in every cell,
but her muscles are locked,
She cannot flee to safety.
She knows there will be no safety until she
knows what is under the surface,
and she knows that she will never
know as long as she sits there.
She sits.
And sits.
And sits.
She goes limp and allows herself to fall,
trusting,
Trusting in what?
That others will help her navigate the reef?
That she will remember how to descend
and ascend on her own?
She does not know.
But she trusts nonetheless.

The Flower

I saw you in a magnolia today.
I knew it was you.
You were off by yourself,
a beautiful pure white,
waiting for me to notice you,
to pick you up,
to know you are thinking of me.
I don't want a flower.
I want you.
But, without you, I'll treasure the flower.

He sits beside her,
Uninvited.
She senses his presence,
familiar now.
She feels his heat.
She hears his breath.
She doesn't want him there.
She slides down the sofa.
He slides down, too.
He is there, with her,
invited or not.
She finally turns to him and asks him to leave.
He does not move.
She gets irritated and tries to push him away.
He does not budge or react.
She screams at him to leave, just leave.
He is impassive.
She cries.
She pleads.
She reasons.
She promises.
He stays.
Quietly.
Firmly.
He is there.
She accepts his presence.

She sighs.
She relaxes.
He is there.
She can be here while he is there,
next to her
Somehow she knows he will always be there.

B Movie

I've been cast in a B movie,
wincingly reciting clichéd lines,
and I don't even recall auditioning for the role.

Action!
Furrowed brow,
words of sorrow,
words of hope,
cut,
repeat.

Others have played this role before,
putting in their time,
memorizing their lines,
wanting to do well enough,
to land a better part.

My mind wanders,
and I sleepwalk through the scene,
then I remember that it's important to do it right,
not for this film,
but for my future.

Survival

I can handle this.
At first it seems like a tenuous thought,
but when I look back,
I see
that I always handled whatever came.
Not gracefully,
not efficiently,
but somehow, I handled it.
And I will handle this, too.

Ice

The water swirls with possibility.
It can flow or drip or soak into a fabric.
It can disappear into the air or sink into the ground.
But…
it doesn't do any of those things.
Instead,
molecule by molecule, it arranges itself into neat rows.
until it is solid,
unable to shapeshift any longer.
and it is undeniably an ice cube.
Hard and unyielding,
solid and real.

The Kitchen Floor

He woke up feeling fine.
Now he is in a fetal position sobbing on the kitchen floor.
Nothing happened,
There is nothing special about this day,
but there he is,
on the floor,
not knowing how he got there.
He thinks of all he misses
over and over again.
Sharp pain travels through his body in waves,
as he lies,
unable to gather the strength to move,
not knowing how long he has been there,
or how long he will stay.

Tuning

A lone oboe begins,
with a piercing sob.
Soon others join,
with their own distinct cries,
the cellos,
the flutes,
adding to the swelling commotion,
until reaching an apex,
and slowly fading in reverse,
to silence,
so the beautiful music can begin.

Wrong

It shouldn't have been.
It wasn't time.
It's wrong, wrong, wrong.
It should have come later.
Much, much later.
Then it would have been reasonable.
But now, it is anything but reasonable.
It is a violation of nature.
A disruption of all that should have been.

Reminiscing

A sentimental feeling,
my mind drifting back over the years,
skipping lightly,
like turning pages in an old album,
a slight smile on my lips,
a light furrow of my brow,
with gentle longing,
for what was,
and what never will be.

The Chest

The chest is tightly shut,
with a shiny metal lock.
Objects inside precisely placed,
never to move again.
Unchanging with time,
not decaying or gathering dust,
but not being added to, either.
Nobody looks inside the box,
until there is no one who even remembers what is in there.

Spirit

I was never sure of anything I couldn't touch or see.
But since you have gone I can feel
what I can't touch or see.
I don't know what it is,
but I am certain that it's there.

I can tap into it,
at times,
and it will support me.
I think of you,
a hummingbird appears,
a baby has your green eyes,
and I sense it.

It's in you.
It's in me.
It's in all of us.
And it is outside of us at the same time.
Everywhere.
Always.
If only I remember to notice.

My Friend

She was her own unique mixture
of understated humor
and loving spirit
and sharp intelligence
and deep-seated gentleness
and sincere empathy
and delightful creativity
and effortless grace.
She was my friend.
I will never know another like her,
but am forever blessed by knowing her.

The Farm

I have seen death on the farm.
Little kittens born,
living out their lives and quietly dying.
Coyotes stalking chickens,
taking them suddenly in the dark of night.

I have seen lives come and seen lives go.
Sometimes timely,
sometimes not.
Each life its own,
and yet each a part of the whole.
A rhythm to the coming and going,
a pulse with no beginning and no end,
bursts of joy and sadness in a never-ending beat.

Today

Today is a good day,
bright and golden.
Today I can breathe,
and think,
and move,
and talk,
and laugh,
and smile,
Maybe tomorrow will be different,
but today is a good day.

The Storm

A few scattered clouds merge together
until the sky is a light gray.
It turns darker and darker until
what is overhead looms like wet concrete.
The clouds swell with pressure until
they burst,
releasing torrents of liquid intensity.
The winds roar,
the trees sway,
the birds scurry back to the shelter of their nests.
The storm soaks the earth
and rocks everything above it,
while the green plants hold on by their roots
to the safety of the ground.

As the deluge eases,
it turns into a steady rain,
beating down on all below,
relentlessly.
Slowly, slowly easing
into a fine shower
that lazily remains
until a single ray of light pokes through the clouds,
signaling the end of the storm.

Inside Out

It's sharp and jagged on the inside,
calm and smooth outside.
Don't they know?
The inside is pleading, screaming,
The outside is placid, unaware.

Slowly, the inside bleeds out,
And, even more slowly, the outside seeps in,
Until they are one.

Gone

The quiet presence that was his
is no longer.
The memories in his mind
locked there forever.
It all disappeared with his last breath.
The way he smiled,
sideways.
The way he loved
a parade
and me.
Gone.

After Death

Where does life go
when it leaves a body?
Does it float upward
to space?
Is it in the air
around me?
Does it return to the earth
to grow into a new life?
Or is it in me now?

Hidden Danger

Tripwires and landmines
surrounding me,
hidden beneath the deceptively calm surface,
in unknown places,
ready to strike:
a friend's birthday party,
a news magazine arriving in the mail,
driving past the hospital,
irises blooming in the yard.
Each exerts a little bit of pressure,
on a trigger that is way too sensitive,
causing detonation,
an explosion of uncontrolled sorrow
in my eyes and in my heart.

The Sun

The light
is peeking through the clouds.
Sometimes the clouds pass over the sun,
and everything goes dark.
And then the sun peeks out again,
coming and going,
coyly playing with me.
Offering the possibility that
it will shine unimpeded.
Of course it will.
I just don't know when.

They

They are here with me,
perched on my shoulder,
whispering those little comments I know so well.
They are pleased when I am happy,
concerned when I'm upset.
Most of all,
they want me to get on with my life.
They gently prod me whenever I look back,
telling me not to look at them,
but to look ahead.
I trust that they will be there,
silently watching my life unfold.

The One

The one who got my paper in the morning
and my mail in the evening,
The listener who heard all my troubles,
The only person who knew that I like
yellow roses, but not red,
The person who held my past.
My co-parent.
My nurse.
My handyman.
My reassurance.
The one who understood why I like my cousin,
even if he irritates the rest of the world.
The one who could mix my daiquiri just the way I like it,
and the one who would never throw out the shirt I hated.
The one who held my future.
My companion.
My witness.
My love.

The River

I thought I was climbing a mountain,
but I was really floating down a river.
It's just as scary.
I'm just as much at the whim of nature,
and at the mercy of the terrain,
but I don't have to try so hard.
I can float.
I can look around at the oak trees passing by,
see what's around the next bend if I wait,
rest while I travel,
and, if I trust, I will be carried to where I was meant to be.

Softness

Aching for softness,
sharp edges filed round,
steel melting into liquid,
piles of quilts to sink into,
the breath of a sleeping baby,
surrounded by warmth,
smooth, spongy, supple,
suspended in time,
is where I want to be.

Wine

Sharp and acrid, the wine
will be put into the dark cave for a while,
to rest,
and dull its bitter finish,
until it can be brought into the light of day,
and be examined,
and sipped,
in measured bits,
glass by glass,
bottle by bottle,
and we can revel in the symphony of its beauty,
and share tales together deep into the night.

Near

She is vague, but she's close.
I'm losing the exact timbre of her laugh,
the sharpness of her nose,
the lilac smell of her hair,
but I feel her, nonetheless.
She is with me always.
Sometimes I forget,
but then I turn to her,
and she is there.

Sailing

Sailing on my small boat,
I'm cozy and snug in the cabin,
everything locked into place,
rocking gently with the waves,
predictably,
back and forth.

Will I dare to venture out,
unfurl the sails,
and race across the open water once more,
into the vast and unknowable distance?

Who Am I?

Who am I without you?
Am I still a spouse
without a partner?
Am I still funny
if only you were laughing?
Am I still the courageous one
if no one else witnesses it?
Am I still an in-law
without you as our connection?
Am I still loved
if no one brings me tulips?
Am I still me
if I am forever without you?

I no longer know.

Walking

I have been in bed so long,
I don't know if I can stand.
I take a deep breath and get up,
wobbly and unsteady at first,
knees threatening to buckle,
But the longer I stand, the firmer I feel,
until I dare to take a single step,
and now I am walking,
hesitantly, but definitely walking,
knowing I can come back to bed,
and rise again.

My Heart

Everyone sees me as happy,
not knowing that behind my fragile, brittle skin,
deep down beneath my bones and muscles,
my heart is sobbing.

Healing, no.
Accommodating, yes.
Moving on, no.
Living with, yes.
I shout "no" to anything that says I am leaving you behind.
I whisper "yes" to bringing you with me.
Changed,
but real.

The Light

It has been so dark,
I have not been able to see farther than my foot,
for a long, long time.

I could see backward in time,
and I could see now,
but not forward.

But the darkness has lifted,
I look up,
and see what lies ahead.

It does not look so bad,
not all of it.
Maybe I could go there.

Into the light.

Your Life

What are you going to do with your house,
now that the foundation has crumbled?
Are you going to let it decay,
while time and weather carry it toward the grave?
Or are you going to rebuild,
more magnificently,
a palace that wouldn't have been possible,
without the footprint of the one that came before?

Settling In

The Persian is settling in for the night.
It is winter outside,
but the cat has found a warm spot at the foot of the bed.

He stretches and scratches,
and lowers his body onto the soft white blanket,
letting the folds envelop his fur.

He closes his eyes,
for a long nap.
He will awaken in the spring.

The Myth

Closure.
Healing.
Resolution.
They are not to be.
I slowly awaken to this truth.
Perhaps integration.
I will take this loss forward with me,
into my new life,
in every cell of my body,
a part of who I am,
and who I always will be,
from this moment on.

Snow

Snow can fall softly,
carpeting the landscape with an enchanting blanket.
Or it can be hard and icy,
full of danger.
It can be whipped around by the wind,
seeping into cracks and clothing,
cold and wet.
From behind a window,
it can be thrilling and dramatic.

Snow can be many different things.

Depending on the season,
the weather,
your protection,
your mood,
your point of view.

Where Is She?

Where is she?
Is she all around me?
Does she wait for important moments to check in?
Is she in the ray of sunshine that settles
on the table while we are eating?
Or is she the eagle I see soaring above the lake?
Sometimes I can feel her with me.
Other times I think I'm imagining her.
Her signs are obtuse.
Couldn't she just be a little more obvious?
For me?
Or maybe she is obvious.
Maybe she's always here,
and I just need to see with my heart.

The Tiny Being

There's a tiny, tiny being hiding somewhere behind my heart.
He is light on his feet, scampering
away every time he is spotted.
He knows he isn't wanted, so he makes
himself nearly invisible,
as expected.
But the little one finds it hard to stay still
Because inside he's jumping for joy,
bursting with happiness and relief.
Not wanting to be seen,
yet yearning to be seen.
Embarrassed,
Ashamed,
Exuberant,
Guilty,
He exists,
whether he is acknowledged or not.

Home

Where is your home now?
Where is the familiar and the good?
Is it outside of yourself,
causing you to wander and search?
Or is it inside yourself,
waiting to be discovered?
What will it be made of?
Stonework solid enough to withstand a gale?
Or delicate rice paper flexing in the gentle wind?
How will you know you are home?
By the people waiting for you when you open the door?
Or by the inner knowing that this is,
and always was,
your home?

A Life

Snapshots of a life,
tender to view.
Comfort and pain,
in equal measure.

Acknowledgments

As with all books, so many people made it possible for this volume to come into being. Although I had the idea suddenly, and the poems often popped into my head fully-formed in the middle of the night, the groundwork had been laid prior to that, and a great cleanup crew followed behind.

This book could not have been created were it not for the incredible work of professionals who have devoted their lives to understanding and helping those who are grieving a loss. Some of the most important influences for me have been Dr. George Bonanno, Dr. Therese Rando, Dr. John Jordan, Dr. J. William Worden, Dr. Kenneth Doka and Dr. Robert Neimeyer. I also learned important lessons in how to be with people in pain from Dr. Marshall Rosenberg and Dr. Tara Brach. A heartfelt thank-you for all you have done to ease pain in the world, both directly and by sharing your research and wisdom with people like me.

I also offer heartfelt appreciation to my mentors and colleagues at Hospice of Santa Cruz County, and those in my local therapist community. These include, but definitely aren't limited to, Elaine Cashman, Anna Paganelli, Catherine Marcotte, and every single one of the grief support interns I have had the honor of working with. I have never known people with such big hearts, and I have learned from each one of you.

This volume is much improved due to the work of my skillful editors, Andrea Hope and Valerie Brooks. I knew nothing about writing poetry and you shepherded me through with equal measure of corrections and encouragement.

Thank you to my clients who place your trust in me, allow me to learn with you, and inspire me daily with your courage. I am constantly awed by your willingness to move toward the hard places, driven by your desire to grow, be authentic, and support yourselves in order to live out your unique potentials.

I appreciate you, Jennifer Young, for being at my side for every step of my journey, empathizing with the hard parts and laughing at the absurdities, while always understanding and encouraging me. And thank you to Doug for your unwavering support through our personal journey of heartbreak and hope. There's no one I'd rather travel with.

About the Author

Kara Bowman is a licensed Marriage and Family Therapist who specializes in grief and trauma. She has a part-time private practice in Santa Cruz, California. Kara traveled a long, winding road to arrive at her current profession. She began with an MBA and a career in finance, opened a large, award-winning child development center, worked in non-profit administration, and homeschooled her three children before becoming an NVC Compassionate Communication Trainer.

Just as Kara's children were leaving home and she was settling into her life, her family was hit with a nearly unbelievable wave of illnesses and deaths in a five-year period. Once Kara found her feet again, she knew she was driven to help others who were experiencing grief, loss and trauma.

Kara returned to school to earn a Masters in Counseling Psychology, and completed her internships primarily in hospice grief counseling. Kara is a Certified Grief Counselor (AAGC), a Certified Clinical Trauma Professional (IATP), and a Certified Thanatologist (the study of death and dying; ADEC). Research and knowledge are growing in the field of grief, and Kara's passion is to help create a culture which is more compassionate and helpful toward those who are grieving (which will eventually be all of us).

Kara is dedicated to her career and community through her practice and volunteer work. Although she always uses empathy as a foundation for her grief work, she tries to individualize her approach in order to give each client what they most need at that moment in time. This includes ritual, poetry, meditations and visualizations, along with talking. Kara loves sharing her knowledge of how to grieve, and how to support grievers, by volunteering at Hospice, giving talks to public groups and training therapists. In the summer of 2020, the California Association of Marriage and Family Therapists honored Kara's practice with a Spotlight in *The Therapist* magazine.

Kara lives in Santa Cruz, California, near the redwoods and the ocean, with her husband. She loves to read, write, walk, do pilates, cook, visit with friends and family, and try to make people laugh. She is very thankful her three grown children all live on the west coast.

russell. robertson smith
Con